THERE ARE ONLY

TWO

RELIGIONS

IN THE WHOLE WORLD

Religious Confusion vs.
The Black Spiritual Rise

B Y   A K I L

Printed in The United States of America
International Standard Book Number #1-56411-116-4

Published by Nia Communications/Press
p.o.b. 5631• saint louis, missouri 63121
"communicating with a purpose"

First Printing February 1995
Second Printing June 1996
Third Printing September 1997
Fourth Printing, December 1998

Cover Design By: Timothy Oriki & Mr. Akil

Toll-Free Order Line 1-888-244-5770
w h o l e s a l e & r e t a i l b o o k s e l l e r s

Nia Comm./Press
" c o m m u n i c a t i n g   w i t h   a   p u r p o s e "

TABLE OF CONTENTS

DEDICATION

...these writings are dedicated to the mental rise of the Blackman and Blackwoman.

Also, this work is given in honor to the loving memory of Mr. E.L. Rivers. "Your great teaching legacy lives on."

T H E
F O R E W O R D

"Religion", as it is known today, has become an enemy to the mental rise of the Blackman and Blackwoman, especially here in America. This is because "so-called" religion has been used as an oppressive tool to totally destroy the natural "spirituality" that is innately born into every precious Black child. And we must learn that this innately born "natural spirituality" and "organized religion" are two totally different things.

Our historical oppressors have used "so-called" religion to stupify our own personal intellect by teaching us white supremacy with a "religious title" stamped on it. And it is because we are a "spiritual" people by nature, that we were naively succeptable to this deceit.

Well all of this wickedness inflicted against us has left us "Religiously Confused", "Religiously Divided", and mentally/spiritually destroyed. We have been so mentally wounded with this religious confusion that many of our intellectuals find it more intelligent to embrace "atheism" (the belief in no God at all).

But how can you disbelieve in the reality of yourself? How can you disbelieve in that which is the core essence of yourself? How can you disbelieve in you?

Well in truth, we all have been made into "atheists" because we have no belief nor "con-fideence" in Black self. This has been the arch-deceiver's plan all along...to divide, conquer, and confuse you and I of the innate divine power of our own supreme being.

So, let us not waste any more time. Let us now begin to wage war on this cancerous ignorance that has been inoculated into our minds by the wicked hand of our historical oppressors...It's time, don't you think?

THERE ARE ONLY

TWO

RELIGIONS

IN THE WHOLE WORLD

Religious Confusion vs.
The Black Spiritual Rise

"I AM A JEW, I AM A CHRISTIAN, AND I AM A MUSLIM"

Brothers and Sisters, the world in which we live today is a confused one. And the title of this essay is not meant to confuse us anymore than we have already been confused. This is simply an effort to reverse the religious confusion that has plagued our minds for much too long.

Listen closely now. The confusion of our minds is the rooted source to all of the confusion in our lives. The thoughts of our individual minds directly projects the image and events of our individual lives before us. Read that again please. <u>The state or condition of our thinking at</u>

2

this very moment, is immediately influencing, controlling, and producing the state or condition of our living at this very moment. Oh, that is powerful, if we deeply understand.

So, all of this means that before any type of "confusion" can enter into the physical/material existence of our lives, it must first be born as a "confused" thought pattern through the mental womb of our minds. Do you understand?

Every single thing in material existence was at one time only an idea or a thought in a mind.

Everything of confusion, conflict, corruption, and chaos that we see before us "today", was once just a corrupt idea or chaotic thought pattern in a brain/mind "yesterday", before it became manifest to this world in the form of all this mischief and bloodshed. To put it simply, you got to "think" like a fool before you begin to "act" a fool. That is the pattern. That is the way it works. Do you clearly understand? Okay.

Well, if we clearly understand the previous point, this automatically tells us that everything of peace, love, righteousness and wisdom, will also have to first come to birth through the portal way of a mind as well. And we, you and I, are now beginning to bring forth the "idea" of peace first, that it may eventually become a concrete living "reality" in our everyday lives. It is the cycle of all creation. Think about that Blackman and Blackwoman.

(STOP-THINK)

Now, let us get straight to the point of our discussion to see how all of this links together. How did this religious confusion come to be? What is the ultimate root of all of this religious division?

Okay, okay, okay, so you call yourself a "Black Jew (or Hebrew)". And you over there call yourself a "Black Muslim", while you right over here call yourself a "Black Christian". Right?

Okay, so now what? Now what? I ask you that because you and I both know that no matter what "you" may call "yourself", to most of the racist sick-minded people in this country and abroad, we are all considered to be nothing but a bunch of no-good "Black Niggers"! Right? You know that's right. We must tell the truth here where it needs to be told, so let's listen.

While we are all standing around arguing with one another about who has got the "true" God, and who is going to the "true" heaven, we are all catching "true" hell from this "true" devil. And this is "truly" a shame. Think about it Black people.

Now, putting all egos aside, don't you think that it is well past due for us to wake-up from this childishness? Don't you think that it is past the time for us to wake-up from all of this foolishness? Yes, well I think so too.

We have over-slept, even though the alarm of truth has been sounding in our ears for decades already. But you know that a deaf man can't hear, and a dumb man can't understand what it is that he has heard. And since our enemies have trained us to be blind, deaf, and dumb, we continue to remain deeply within our ignorant slumber. Right? Come on. Let's read on.

We are not fully awakened to the reality around us. No. This is exactly why we are still standing right in the middle of Hell arguing amongst ourselves about which direction leads to Heaven. Meanwhile, this little devil is laughing himself to death at us fools, as he further instigates the confusion that he originally orchestrated to divide us from one another. Yes, this is true.

The reason that we are now so confused and divided about which way is the right way to get to "heaven", or achieve salvation, is because we are seeking advice and guidance from our historical enemies. Think about this now.

Why should our historical enemies, who have historically made our lives a "living hell" for centuries upon centuries, turn around and give us the <u>accurate</u> directions of how to get to a "living heaven"? Why should they do this all of a sudden? No, a better question is, "Why would we expect them to do this all of a sudden?" What indication do we have that they would truly do this for you and I?

Why should we believe that someone who has intentionally served us "death" for so many centuries, would all of a sudden want to serve us "life"? It is crazy to think that an evil person, who has committed such world-wide devilishment, would give us the accurate directions to the path of Righteousness! Wake-up beloved Blackpeople! How can they give you directions to a place where they have never been?!?...can't be done.

Listen! Listen! Listen! Don't you see what has happened to us? Don't you know who you are? Don't you know your wonderful value? Do you? Well? Huh? Hmmm?

What is it about you Blackpeople that would cause other people to feel such a fanatical need to spend so much time, money, planning, effort, and energy to prevent your rise? Who are you? What is your potential? Blackman and Blackwoman do you know who you are? Are you sure about that?

Listen!...just listen. Way, way, way back-when, a long, long time ago, we knew the true path of God. Way back into our greatest ancient civilizations we knew the clear path of God and we taught this divine wisdom in our great universities of that day. People traveled from all over the earth to study these divine sciences. We knew the true reality of God and knew the clear path to God. We were divinely awakened. We had the map in our hands, because we illuminated the blue-print. This is our ancient history. Study up on that.

Well, to make a long, long, long, long story short, there were some people who could not seem to cognitively grasp the higher scientific concepts taught at our universities that would advance them to the higher teachings of moral civilization. So out of their impatience to study and learn step by step, they began to savagely attack our people, steal from our universities, and burn our libraries of divine knowledge. They fell from the grace of the God. They eventually invaded and brutally conquered our ancient lands over time. And they then shipped us into slavery, so that "they" could now become the builders of civilization around the world. But how can those who have yet to be civilized, teach the arts and sciences of civilization? Good question.

They wanted to imitate our historical legacy of greatness, so much so, that they savagely knocked us in the head, took the book of knowledge from our hands, and sat down upon our throne while parading around in our righteous garments. Ain't that something? And in order for them to maintain their power for a set period of time, they had to strip us of our power by making you and I blind, deaf, and dumb to the knowledge of our true selves and our true history. I know that you can see this.

Yes, and as you already know, our Black forefathers and foremothers were raped and stripped naked of their names, knowledge, wisdom, and dignity to be brought into a strange land amongst a strange people onto the wicked slave plantation.

Our people were then put onto breeding farms where they were forced to sexually intercourse, in order to produce as many Black (slaves) babies as physically possible. These babies were immediately shipped-off to separate plantations upon birth, so that the wise knowledge of the parents could not be passed on to the young Black brains.

After our foreparents had exhausted their ability to physically produce children, and after they had been thoroughly drained and raped of their knowledge, they were brutally murdered in cold Black blood! They were ruthlessly murdered by beasts in human form that had taken on the mind and heart of a devil. And like the scripture says, as a man thinketh in his heart, so is he. But we will leave that alone...for right now.

Well, needless to say, we as being those helpless new-born children no longer had our original parents. They had been killed. We now had the slave-master as our foster-parents. And, under the guidance of these foster-parents, we were purposely raised to be ignorant to the knowledge of our true selves by these wicked oppressors. The more ignorant we are, the better servants and slaves we are to them. They had to murder our minds first, in order to make us their voluntary servants. This is how we are manipulated even today.

Of course we were never told that we were actually the descendants of Black Kings, Black Queens, Black Gods, and Black Goddesses of an ancient collective Black Genius Mind that exists eternally throughout all space and time. No, of course not. The slavemaster has lied to us from the very beginning.

We were taught to be ignorant, submissive, "slave-niggers" and "live-in hoars" for the lustful pleasure and greedy profit of a sick-minded slavemaster.

Our minds were violently raped. Our self-esteem and self-worth were completely destroyed. And we were taught to hate every aspect of our Black selves. We had been reduced to the mental level of a savage and were taught that we descended from savages in Africa. But it is now very obvious that we were actually being taught savagery by the true savage in person.

And so now, it is in this state of savagery that we have remained for all too long...left in this state of confused mental death. This is so sad, but this is so true. The painful truth must be told and accepted as truth, for us to eventually grow beyond the pain. (Pause-Think)

Let us move on. So now, these same evil-hearted enemies saw it prosperous to further capitalize off of our destroyed state of mind.

They now want to take it upon themselves to show us the path of God and righteousness, since we are living such a hard, punishing, life of misery. You know, ...they told us that we were cursed Black heathens who needed the lilly-white, blue-eyed Jesus to come and save us of our sinful savagery. Yes, and we naively, therefore whole-heartedly took their guidance as truth; Even though it seems more like we are actually that "Black Jesus" who is being unjustly nailed to the cross of punishment, pain, poverty, and persecution by the political powers of this present day. Is this just a coincidence? It seems as if we are the ones asking, "Father, hast thou forsaken me?"

It is no wonder that we have not found God or salvation yet, considering the fact that we have taken our instructions from those who act as an enemy to The God, in their rebellion to righteousness.

Remember that this historical enemy had stolen the book of The Knowledge of God from us in the first place. But to further confuse us in our mental state of ignorance, he has torn the book into separate individual pieces and placed different names on each individual section, in different individual languages. Look at it.

He is so wickedly intelligent that he has fooled the majority of the world's population into his religious confusion, but especially us, the now mentally dead Original Black People of the Earth. Isn't that something?

We, The Original Black Nation, of whom The God worked through to author all of this divine wisdom in the first place, are now the people who have been the most wickedly deceived. We who once held the book in our heads, hearts, and hands are now childishly arguing over the different separated pieces of that same one book. What a shame.

Some of us have a Torah (old testament). Some of us have a Bible. Some of us have a

Quran. Some of us have a book of (Black Egyptian) Kemitic Hieroglyphics. And some of us have a book of Metaphysics, while all of us are arguing over who has the right book.

But listen, the comprehensive point is that we are all holding the different pages to the same ONE book! These are all scriptures from the same ONE book which was authored by the same ONE God! All divine revelation is revealed by the ONE God! All that you see in creation is authored and created by the ONE rooted source!

The ONE God is the blessed tie that binds all divine righteousness and divine wisdom together! We must now understand who we are so that we do not further fall prey to the 'divide and conquer' tactics of our enemies anymore than we already have. It is about that time, don't you think? Yes, I think so too.

May I ask you a question, Blackman and woman? What would happen if we stopped looking to our enemies for spiritual guidance, and started to look toward the One True God rooted within the nature of our own true selves? What if we started to realize that all of these books of knowledge are in fact just pieces to the same ONE puzzle? What if we realized that all of this divine wisdom was originally authored through our own forgotten ancient ancestors of divine? What if we started to realize who we really are?

Well, who are we? We are the Original Black People from which all others were born. This is why we are called the Mothers and Fathers of Civilization. We have given birth to all, and therefore all is contained within the origin of our fertile Blackness. All others are yet different manifested attributes of what is contained within the ONE original archetype. Do you understand?

With a study of nature, we find that the whole spectrum of "individual colors" have come from the collective origin of "Black", and it is there that they all must eventually return. So within the collective Blackness, there is no "red", no "green", no "blue", no "yellow", no "white", or no "purple". Once returned to their state of origin they are all ONE. They are all "Black".

Black is the collective whole of the entire color spectrum manifesting simultaneously at ONE time. Black only manifests itself into many different colors, that it may gain a better knowledge of the contents of self. We are all in tribes and families that we may know one another, and therefore know self. Can you see the parallels?

Well, in the "<u>Original</u> Blackman and Blackwoman", there is no "Jew", no "Christian", no "Muslim", no "Buddhist", no "Egyptologist", or no "MetaPhysicist". We are 'all-ah-that' at one time. All of these different fields of study have originated from the same ONE school of thought, which was born from our ancient Black collective consciousness.

A Torah, a Bible, a Quran, a book of Ancient Hieroglyphics, a book of Chinese philosophy, a book of Metaphysics, or any book of mathematics and science, all have their common rooted origin in a fertile Black seam of divine consciousness. Okay? Are you hearing this?

Listen closely. **You** are that Black seam of consciousness, and that Black seam runs deeply within your heart, mind, collective sub-conscious memory, and DNA genetic coding. Yes. And the reason that we are so religiously confused today, is because we have let other people define us according to these recent johnny-come-lately surface level religious titles, names, and labels!!!

But wait! See, **you** are much, much, much, deeper than that! **You** are that essence from which all of these religions have come forth. **You** are that original mind and that original heart of spirituality from which all of these spiritual descriptions have derived. Yes.

You can not limit me, an Original Blackman, to a surface level religious title! Please! I **am** the Muslim, the Jew (or Original Hebrew), the

Christian, the Egyptologist, the MetaPhysicist, and everything else all at the same time! I **am** all of this by nature! Yes this is true! I **am** of the Original Black Nation. I **am** the origin. I **am**.

The Awakened Original Blackman and Blackwoman understands that the root definition of the word "<u>Muslim</u>" only means "one who is in submission to the will of God". That is our nature. The root definition of the word "<u>Jew</u>" only means "one who is circumcised of the heart". That is our nature. The root definition of the word "<u>Christian</u>" only means "one who seeks to be crystallized into the mind of The Christ (or the mind of God)" That is our nature. Do you clearly understand?

I **am** an Original "<u>Muslim</u>" because I am "<u>one who is in submission to the will of God</u>".

I **am** an Original "<u>Jew</u>" because I am "<u>one who is circumcised of the heart</u>".

I **am** an Original "<u>Christian</u>" because I am "<u>one who seeks to be crystallized into the mind of The Christ (or the mind of God)</u>".

I am an Original "Egyptologist" because I am "the Black seed to that great ancient civilization of Kemet; and every divine Black God and divine Black Goddess that has ever existed, is wrapped-up within the sub-conscious mind of my third-eye awaiting the right stimulus to awaken and exhibit the Ma'atic balance of supreme peace and supreme power of ancient divine."

I am an Original "MetaPhysicist" because "I understand that to study the higher scientific laws of the outer physical world, while focusing on the complimenting interactions of 'energy and matter' throughout our universe, will assist us in understanding the relative complimentary interactions of 'energy and matter' within our own internal being, that will guide us toward the alignment of our lives with the divine nature in which we were originally created, so that this harmonious alignment will bring peace to our total atmosphere or sphere of atoms." Yes, **I am** all of that! Most importantly this means that,

"You are all of that!" We are the ORIGIN-AL!!!
The Origin.

\- \- \- \- \- \- \- \- \- \- \- \- \- \- \- \- \- \- \- \-

The root essence of God is within you. And
you are made in the image and likeness of The
God. The Unseen animates that which is seen.
You and I are all gods and goddesses but yet
children of That Most High God...the sons and
daughters of our Creator.

So, don't you ever try to divide me from you
or you from me based on some petty religious
title! No! No! No! We are bigger than any little
recent religious title! You and I were here before
religion had a title, brother! Back in the day, we
did not even need so-called "religion" as we
have it today, sister! We just lived a twenty-four
hour day of constant spirituality.

Back then, we didn't need to seek refuge from
the devil's world into any temple, church,
synagogue or mosque, because there was no

devil's world yet. The world belonged to the righteous.

The entire earth was "our" temple and "our" prayer was the spiritual way in which "we" lived and loved "our" lives. The living of a righteous life was an act of worship and gratitude to The Most High God. What better way can you show honor and respect to a righteous God, other than to live a sincerely righteous life? This is the one lifestyle that we all originated from and where we all shall return as One. Remember that.

It is the recently born six-thousand year old young childish Caucasian that has been used to instigate and perpetuate all of this Religious confusion and division in the earth. You need not hate him for this, as you need not hate any rebellious child. You correct and curb the child's behavior by asserting your authority as The Parent. He needs guidance. And it is the eternally old wise mind of God awakened in you who will reproduce Spiritual Clarity, and whom will ad-minister The Guidance.

"You" are not really the descendants of any of these recent prophets and messengers of the wisdom of God. The Original people are the Mothers and Fathers of these prophets and messengers of God. You are the righteous authors of the ancient wisdom that sent them all forth. But we are now asleep to the awareness of self. We are not aware of the contents of self. Greatest is thee that is in you, than thee that enslaves you.

Since we are dead to the knowledge of our true selves, our enemy can come amongst us to easily divide us and conquer us. We started off as one collective solid unit in the family of God, until an enemy came in and re-named all of us into individual separate little splinter groups. United we stood, while divided we have fallen. The rebellious child authored this chaos and confusion so that he could gain power, control, and dominion over the minds of the world's population.

It is easy to conquer a whole community of people one house at a time. So, the child took it upon himself to divide God's community apart one house at a time, by giving each house a separate name; **"Presbyterian"**, **"Shiite"**, **"Falasha"**, **"Catholic"**, **"Orthodox"**, **"Episcopalian"**, **"Sunni"**, **"Hebrew"**, **"Lutheran"**, **"Moor"**, **"Baptist"**, **"Ahmadiyya"**, **"Buddhist"**, **"Hindu"**, **"Fahami"**, **"Jew"**, **"Christian"**, **"Muslim"**, **"Black-Nationalist"**, **"Pan-Africanist"**, **"Black Mason"**, **"Black Shriner"**, **"Democrat"**, **"Republican"**, **"Upper-Class"**, **"Middle-Class"**, **"Lower-Class"**, **"tall"**, **"short"**, **"fat"**, **"skinny"**, **"male"**, **"female"**, **"light-skinned"**, **"dark-skinned"**, **"Crips"**, **"Bloods"**, **"Watts"**, **"Compton"**, **"Bronx"**, **"Brooklyn"**, **"North Side"**, **"South Side"**, **"East Coast"**, **"West Coast"**, **"negro"**, **"nigger"**, **"colored"**, **"African-American"**, **"Afro-American"**, or anything else that could be used to divide us apart!!! This is truly a shame!

See, we can't forget that our Motherland, that is now called "Africa", used to be ONE great united empire. But after the deceit, trickery, manipulation, and deception of these european (caucasian) exploiters, the land became fractionalized into little scattered colonized countries of what once was United.

The portugese, the french, the italian, the british and other european "exploiters" (even though they call themselves "explorers") got together in front of a map and carved-up Africa like a pie.

Now Africa is called, **"Nigeria"**, **"Zaire"**, **"Sudan"**, **"Gabon"**, **"Angola"**, **"Namibia"**, **"Libya"**, **"South Africa"**, **"Zimbabwe"**, 'Saudi Arabia" (after they dug out the suez-canal to separate N.E. Africa from the whole and called it the Middle East), **"Zambia"**, **"Mozambique"**, **"Ethiopia"**, **"Somalia"**, **"Ghana"**, **"Liberia"**, **"Senegal"**, **"Guinea"**, **"Kenya"**, **"Uganda"**, **"Madagascar"**, **"Botswana"**, **"Morocco"**,

**"Algeria", "Tunisia", "Niger", "Mali", "Egypt",
Etc., Etc., Etc.!!!!!!!**

Can you believe that!? That is just like
somebody coming into your family reunion, and
giving every individual person a different last
name. Pretty soon there would be no more
family reunions, because after a while you
wouldn't know who was related to who????

These deceitful little enemies colonized our
people into little separated groups (or countries)
and then taught the children of each group to
speak an entirely different european language
from one another so that unity could never have
the possibility of ever being replaced in the
future!!!

Do you understand? Do you understand? Do
you now understand the wicked science of the
"divide-and-conquer" tactic that your enemy
has used on you? Was it made clear enough?
Can you see this, Black people??? Read all of
that over again for a deeper understanding.

Please pay close attention. So now, God's

whole community has been fighting and killing one another over these separate little petty names, labels, and titles that this little devil has divided us with. Our frame of thinking has become so ignorantly immature and shallow.

While we are out in the streets, highways, and bi-ways fighting one another over these petty little titles, this little devil has taken over all of our houses and therefore our entire community.

So much so that now, when we get sleepy and tired of ignorantly fighting one another for the day, we have to come back home and pay rent to the enemy of God to stay in our own house.

He has convinced us to pay him for the Earth's water. He has convinced us to pay him for Nature's electricity. He has convinced us to pay him for Our food plus other basic goods and services.

He has even convinced us to pay him taxes plus a monthly lease on some land that has been here since before there was even a such thing as a caucasian. Imagine that?

We are paying him tens and hundreds of thousands of dollars in life-insurance monies, for a life that he did not grant us nor can he insure. We are paying him for "life-insurance", just in case we "die". Now if we are "dead", how well did he "insure" our "life"? Think about it.

We have to pay him to come to birth from our own Mother's womb, as well as pay him thousands of dollars just to be thrown in a 6ft. hole when we die! We have to pay him just to exist on God's Earth! How much were we paying for all of this before? Isn't this a shame? There is no doubt about it. This is a shame.

So what in this living hell are we arguing and fighting about anyway??? Huh??? One person over here saying that they got the "right God"! One person over there saying that they got the "right God"! But from where I'm standing, it is obvious that ain't neither one of you got no God at all, cause you both taking your guidance from the enemy of God! That is why we are so confused now!

Now wait a minute. Wait a minute. I hope that we have not confusingly mis-taken this little rebellious devil for our true God. It is obvious that we don't really know The God, because we have been made so confused. The devil is the instigator of "confusion", and The God is the author of "clarity". So, from whom have we been receiving our guidance??? Well??? Think about this thing.

Listen! Listen! Listen, Most Beloved Blackman and Most Beloved Blackwoman! These words are not given to insult your intelligence. No. They are given to inspire your intelligence, that we all may rise above the tricknology of our common historical enemies. Right now more than ever you and I must realize that God is ONE and God's people are ONE, that we may proceed in ONE synchronized unit.

We are all but branches to the same Black

family tree. And if we make the intelligent decision to stop magnifying the different individual branches of this tree so much, and start to dig within ourselves to find that common root and seed that we all share together, we can all exalt that common fertile Black source from which we all have sprung!!!

Listen closely. *To exalt and illuminate the one rooted seed of a tree, is to exalt and illuminate the entire tree as a whole. You don't water the branches of a tree, you water the rooted seed through which every branch, stem, leaf, nut, and fruit receives it's sustenance!!!* Can you hear this my dear brother and my dear sister.

That rooted seed is the rooted wisdom of our most ancient ancestral divine Black Mothers and Fathers whom are rooted in The God.

So let us right now begin to honor our Beloved Mother and Father, that our days may be long. This little devil never deserved our honor. Give honor where honor is due. Give honor to the one living true God, whose essence is rooted deeply within you. Come on. Let it be Blackman and Blackwoman. Let it be.

Peace Be Unto Us All.

Thank You.

THERE ARE ONLY "TWO" RELIGIONS IN THE WHOLE WORLD!!!

Many people have died, many families have split apart, and many nations have gone to war in "religious confusion". Chaotic superficial walls of division amongst a misunderstanding people have caused much pain. And it all starts from a simple argument, that does not even have to take place.

Two people begin a discussion and all of a sudden you hear, "Well my religion say this and my religion say that!" "Well my prophet say this and my prophet say that!" "Well I got the 'right' God and the 'only' way to salvation!" Have you heard this before? Yeah, me too. Are you sick of this madness? Yeah, me too. Let us now end all of this foolishness once and for all. Okay?

Please listen-up very, very, very, closely. We have all been fighting one another over so-called religious differences that are not even really there. But we can't seem to see that fact, because we have been reduced to such a shallow- minded frame of thinking.

Just because different people have different so-called religions, we think that people are serving different Gods. Right? You hear people saying, "Well my God say this and my God say that!" This is so foolish, because you know that there is but ONE God! And that God ain't just "your God," that God is "our God"! There is only ONE Supreme ONE worthy of all praise. Our ignorance must cease now. It must. It is going to cease. Our ignorance is ceasing right now as we speak to one another.

Please. It does not matter what righteous name that you give to that Supreme One God, or in what language that name is spoken, as long as you know who it is that you are speaking of. We can say "God", "Lord", "Allah", "Ra", "Buddha", "Jah", "Yahweh", "Amen-Ra", "Jehovah", "Ptah", "Obatala", Olodumare" "Heavenly Father", "Mother Universe" or whatever, but regardless to name or language, we are speaking of but One God. And all of the best names are given in honor to that Supreme One God. Can you see this?

So, to argue and fight over a superficial title of the Most High Supreme God is pure ignorant foolishness. It is childish. It is shallow thinking at this critical time.

Understand that it is not just merely knowing the correct "spelling" and "pronunciation" of the "exterior" name of God that will save our lives from wicked destruction. No. But rather it is the "study" of God's "inner heart" and "inner mind" that will exalt us in righteousness toward a healthy mind state and life. **You can shout God's name all day long, but until you begin to**

live God's wisdom, you will continue to be the same fool that you have always been. Let's Wake-Up.
(STOP-THINK)

And don't start talking about, "Well my prophet say this, and my prophet say that!" You need to shut all of that up today. What do you mean when you say "your prophet"? ...as if that particular prophet came into the world to personally teach just you alone. No, this is not your personal tutor. All prophets and all messengers were sent forth from the same ONE God, and therefore their wisdom belongs to "all" of the righteous ones who are wise enough to receive their guidance.

"Your" prophet is "my" prophet and "my" prophet is "your" prophet! They all belong to us! They and their message all come from The ONE God! Can you understand that. It is not hard to understand. Can you put down that shallow pride long enough to embrace the truth that will set us free of this ignorance? Of course you can, so listen.

If you say to me that "Moses" taught the wisdom of God, I want to learn it!

If you say to me that "Jesus" taught the wisdom of God, I want to learn it too!

If you say to me that "Muhammad" taught the wisdom of God, I want to learn it too!

If you say to me that "Confucius" taught the wisdom of God, I want to learn it too!

If you say to me that the "mathematical and scientific principles of this Universe" were designed by the wisdom of God, I want to learn it too!!!

You can't separate yourself from me! You can't separate me from my beautiful Black brother or my beautiful Black sister over some religious label, title, book, or prophet, because it is all just another part of me and another part of you! This is absolutely true.

(PAUSE-THINK)

I was Black and hated because of my Blackness before I even came out of the womb into the light of the sun. You too were Black and hated way before you learned about any prophet or religious title. Right? So what's all this religious confusion, division, hostility, animosity, and rivalry about?

Our shared experience of hatred and oppression, by our mutual enemies, is the common denominator to overcome any petty so-called differences that prevent our unity! Our true struggle is the same.

You are not being persecuted and hated because of your religious title! Your enemy don't believe in no God! You are hated and persecuted for being an Original Blackman and an Original Blackwoman of marvelous creation!

Envy is at the root of their hatred for us, while **ignorance** is at the root of our hatred for our own selves.

Jealousy is at the root of their hatred for us, while **ignorance** is at the root of our hatred for our own selves.

Fearful-insecurity is at the root of their hatred for us, while **ignorance** is at the root of our hatred for our own selves.

Yes, we were all Black and hated before anything else. And that common hatred touches us even while still in the womb.

Our Black Mothers were so brainwashed into this self-hatred of Blackness, that they would pray and hope that their unborn child would be born with lighter colored skin and with european caucasian physical features. Right? You know that I'm telling you the truth.

If the child was not born "light-skinned" or with what they thought was "good-hair", the Mother would be disappointed with the child.

Now of course the child intuitively senses this disappointment. The disappointment of the Mother deeply hurts and scars the child's mind and self-esteem for life. The Black Mother didn't want her babies to be born "too Black".

This sickness of self-hatred penetrated deeply

into the womb as we were biologically forming stage after stage. Therefore we were infected, affected, and afflicted with the illness of racism being steadily woven into every forming fiber of our entire being even before we came into physical birth.

So it is this common experience of pure hatred that we "all" share. And <u>I don't care if you call yourself a "Black Jew", a "Black Christian", or a "Black Muslim", because as soon as somebody calls you a "Black Nigger", you will realize that we are all on the same side!</u> We will immediately unify! Our common oppression is our common reality. We are all in the same boat, and that boat just happens to be a slave-ship navigated by the wicked hand of our common enemy.

Yes, and that common reality will smack you right in the face to awaken you from all of this ignorant "religious confusion" instigated by our enemies. You will then awaken to find out that **there are truly only two authentic living**

religions in this whole wide world. There are only "two". Only two. Just two. Two.

The only two religions in the whole entire world are called the religion of **"RIGHTEOUSNESS"** and the religion of **"WICKEDNESS"**. There is only God's congregation, and the devil's congregation. So, at which temple do you worship? Think about this thing deeply.

Every prophet and/or messenger of <u>God</u> that ever lived taught only ONE Religion of the two. Each prophet or messenger taught us to <u>obey</u> "Righteousness" and to <u>resist</u> "Wickedness". Right? Right. Simple.

Every <u>devil</u> or enemy to God that ever lived taught only ONE Religion of the two. Each devil and enemy taught, manipulated, or encouraged us to <u>obey</u> "Wickedness" and to <u>resist</u> "Righteousness". Right? Right. Simple.

Those, who have served as our enemies, have

taught or mentally conditioned most of us into their rebellious state of mind (or religion of "WICKEDNESS") through tricks, lies, and mind manipulative evil suggestions. Look at the media.

Go and cut on your radio or television right now and tell me if you find anything other than *"sex, money/materialism, and murder"* glaring out at you in some form or another. "These" are the "evil gods" that we are being subliminally persuaded to worship or submit to as gods to guide us, instead of the principles of Righteousness to guide us. Please read that again.

So, regardless to religious title or name, we are all being attacked together. The people who love righteousness are all locked in the same battle with the same wicked manipulative forces. Now, who will make war with this beast?...this beast in human form that is trying to make beasts out of you and I.

See, if I am intelligent and am a lover of

righteousness, I can't care if you say that "your prophet" taught "you" to pray like this, and that "other prophet" taught "them" to pray like that!

I can't care if you say that "your prophet" walked "these" lands and that "other prophet" walked "those" lands!

I can't care if you say that "your prophet" spoke this language, and that "other prophet" spoke that language!

I can't care if you say that "your prophet" wore a long beard, and that "other prophet" shaved his face!!!

Come on now, this childishness has got to stop! Stop letting this enemy deceive us with this superficial way of looking at things. A true love for Righteousness and a true love for Righteous people doesn't allow you to think in that manner.

These prophets and messengers of God came to make us wise, not foolish! If we stopped foolishly arguing and fighting about "How they taught", "Where they taught", and "When they

taught", we might finally learn about "<u>What</u>
They Taught"!!! Isn't that right? Black people,
we have got to stop being so damn silly!!! Let's
talk straight to one another. Come on now. Our
people are dying, and so are we.

Listen...back to the point about all of these
messengers of The God's wisdom.

So, <u>what</u> did they teach??? They <u>all</u> taught
RIGHTEOUSNESS. They <u>all</u> taught the ONE
true religion of the ONE true message of the
ONE true God, which is obedience to
Righteousness! They all taught the SAME ONE
BASIC MESSAGE! Are you listening?!? Do
you hear this? Pay close attention.

They <u>all</u> taught submission to the will of
**TRUTH, RIGHTEOUSNESS, JUSTICE,
PEACE, WISDOM**, or in other words **GOD**.

Oh yes, you should "fully" perceive this. Yes,
we should memorize, internalize, cognitize,
analyze, and deeply realize this point to the
fullest extent of our ability. <u>This</u> <u>is</u> <u>that</u> <u>truth</u>
<u>that</u> <u>will</u> <u>make</u> <u>you</u> <u>free</u> <u>of</u> <u>that</u> "Religious

Confusion".

It is up to "us" to erase all of these unnecessary confusing lines of division drawn by the wicked hand of our common enemy. There is only one true line of division, and that line is to separate the WICKED from the RIGHTEOUS. Get thee to my left, and get thee to my right! (STOP-THINK)

Don't let all of these different little so-called religious customs and religious rituals keep you religiously confused either. No! Be intelligent.

Don't foolishly remain confused after hearing this message. To remain confused, would be voluntary ignorance. Forget these titles and labels. That is the "peripheral" vision, not the "focused" eye of the God. Regardless to all of these religious-titles, religious-rituals, and religious-traditions, there are but Two true religions in this entire Universe. The temple of Righteousness or the temple of Wickedness. It is quite simple.

So, at which congregation will you seek communion? You can't hide behind your self-given surface level religious label or title anymore. We don't want to read the definition of your religious "title" projected from your mouth. We want to read the definite righteous "reality" of your heart and mind projected by your spirit of character (your thoughts and actions).

There is no more Religious Confusion to hide behind. Either you are of your righteous Father, The God...or you are of your wicked father, the little devil. <u>Righteousness or Wickedness</u>. Only two choices. Only two paths to travel. Only two true religions. It is just that simple. It is truly just that simple. That is it.

Now did you clearly hear that Blackman and Blackwoman? Let's put the childishness aside.

Now, how many religions are their in this world? Well? How many? I can't hear you. Go ahead and answer out loud so everybody can hear you.

There are only two; Righteousness or Wickedness. Make your judgment. Choose one. This is our "judgment" day. I pray (strive) that we make the right "judgment".

Peace,
to the seekers
of righteousness.

THE MISSION OF THE ORIGINAL BLACKWOMAN AND THE ORIGINAL BLACKMAN

If you have never had a purpose of mission in your life before, let us dis-cover what that purpose of mission is right now. Here it is.

Were you created by a Divine Creator? Yes. Well, doesn't that make you a divine creation? Yes. If you are a "divine creation", doesn't that automatically give you a "divine purpose"? Yes!

Listen, "YOU AND YOUR LIFE ARE NO ACCIDENT". Did you hear that? I said "YOU

AND YOUR LIFE ARE NO ACCIDENT"! Come on and repeat after me, "YOU-AND-YOUR-LIFE-ARE-NO-ACCIDENT". The God has made no mistake when making you. You are on purpose. Your life has been created on a Purpose, but have you sought out what that purpose is?

Why are you the Original Blackwoman and Original Blackman from which all others were born? Why? Why does this make you the original seed from which all others have sprouted? Why? Why does this make you the Mothers and Fathers of all? Why? And, do these facts give you any special privilege "in" the world? Or do these facts give you a special responsibility "to" the world??? Good question.

What is your duty? Huh? It is your duty to drink in the wisdom of right guidance that your own life may "actually" begin to live. Then, it is your duty to "serve" the entire world population with the wise guidance of The Original Parents. You are the seed of those elders. But deeper than that, you are these elders. And with the knowledge of this fact comes purpose. And with this wisdom comes mission.

For thousands and thousands of years, the world has been guided and ruled by the young off-spring of the Original Black parents, while these black elders lay mentally asleep. The house has been run-down by our immaturely naive rebellious youths, who did not have the respect, patience, nor willingness to learn the wisdom of their Black Mothers and Fathers.

They learned a lot of our "knowledge" but not the righteous "Wisdom" to know how to properly utilize the knowledge they took. Therefore this world has been turned upside-down into a confused chaotic state of mischief, bloodshed and murder. Peace can not be found. And now the entire household is threatened to total doom and total destruction...inside-out.

Wake up from the ignorant mental slumber Original Blackman and Blackwoman! Your rebellious children are destroying the house.

Wake up and put your house back in order, before it is too late. The time is now. Who else is going to do it besides you and I?

\- \-

As the Original Elders we are now coming back home to our original divine mind-state of peace and power, stage by stage. We will heal these many wounds with supreme peace, and we will also discipline much evil with supreme power. Thy will is being done.

We may not be fully awakened or aware that this divine occurrence is taking place, but yet it is. It is The Unseen. It is not unseen because it can not be seen, but only because most refuse to look. The Earth is constantly revolving, but we will never feel it's motion if we never hold still enough to feel it. It goes Un-felt. It goes Un-seen. But yet, it still goes.

Things are evolving. Things are revolving right before our eyes. You and I are right now taking on the heart, spirit, and mind of

Righteousness/Truth/God to further spread and deliver this unifying message, that will destroy the heart, spirit, and mind of wickedness/lies/devil.

This root understanding of truth will destroy all "Religious Confusion" and chaos amongst our people, and eventually the world. The "sincere internalization" of this message will immediately unify our people, that we may be equipped to successfully deliver this message throughout the earth.

The world needs help. The world needs healing. This household yearns for the ancient divinely-wise Guidance of it's Original parents. The household needs to be taught how to honor thy Original Mother and thy Original Father that their days may be long.

But, look at yourself Original Black people. Why should they honor that which is not yet honorable? Good Question. Understand that the only way to raise your family is to raise yourself, Blackman and Blackwoman. Do you want respect, but yet are not an example of that which is respectable?

You and I must first strive to earn our own Self-Respect, which will result in the respect from all others. Can I repeat that please? *"You and I must first strive to earn our own Self-Respect, which will result in the respect from all others."*

Do you understand that clearly? This is the absolute key to our success! Don't just read over that lightly. These words are not being written to entertain nor impress you. This is to save your "life" and mine.

Now, fully ingest this key into your heart; *"You and I must first strive to earn our own Self-Respect, which will result in the respect from all others."*

We gain this Self-Respect by doing the things which <u>agree</u> <u>with</u> that "righteous voice" of our self-conscience, as opposed to <u>rebelling</u> <u>against</u> that "righteous voice" of our self-conscience.

Question: How does one gain Self-Respect?

Answer: **We gain this Self-Respect by doing the things which <u>agree</u> <u>with</u> that "righteous voice" of our self-conscience, as opposed to <u>rebelling</u> <u>against</u> that "righteous voice" of our self-conscience.**

Question: How does one gain Self-Respect?

Answer: **We gain this Self-Respect by doing the things which <u>agree</u> <u>with</u> that "righteous voice" of our self-conscience, as opposed to <u>rebelling</u> <u>against</u> that "righteous voice" of our self-conscience.**

This is the Key Question, that leads to the Key Answer, that leads to your Key Purpose, which will place you on your Key Mission, to approach your Key Destiny. This Self-Respect will drive you to the Self-Realization of your true Self-Potential.

So, rise to this occasion. Rise to this purpose of mission. Rise from mental death unto the abundance of mental life.

And once our Black Nation has breathed in this breath of life for ourselves, let us serve that life to an entire world that has morally and mentally died away.

We will come to give life. We will come to give life, and give it more abundantly. We give life from that Supreme source that was merciful enough to give us life after our mental death. This is our purpose of mission..."to gain life" and then "to give life."

Is this clearly understandable? There is no need for any more of that "religious confusion". Oh no, there is no need for that now. You have now been provided the plain and sure truth. We are now free from the bondage of that confusion, ignorance, and mis-understanding.

You and I are now wise enough to know that, to truly **Praise** Jesus is to truly **Be** as Jesus! To truly **Praise** Muhammad is to truly **Be** as Muhammad! To truly **Praise** Jehovah is to truly **Be** as Jehovah! To truly **Praise** Allah is to truly **Be** as Allah! To truly **Praise** The God is to truly **Be** as The God!

Anything that teaches us to do other than that

is a "Slave-Making Religion"!

Is it more productive for our hands to do The Righteous Actions of God's will, or for our mouths to shout the idle praise of God's name? Which would The God most appreciate??? You think about it. Common-Sense.

Well now, after all of this, what is your purpose Blackman & Blackwoman?

The purpose of The Original Blackman & Original Blackwoman is to place The Ruler of Righteousness back into the Earth, which will cause peace and the healing of wounds.

Your purpose is to crush the wicked and exalt the righteous...to bring freedom to those who have only known bondage...to bring justice to those who have only known injustice...to bring wisdom to those who have only known ignorance.

Oh "yes sir" and "yes ma'am", that is your purpose brother and sister. This means "You"...Yes, "You". What else is there for a Son or Daughter of God to do???...but serve the will of their Father, which is also the essence of their own righteous will, if they are truly of their Righteous Father?

This is the purpose for **your** living. So, are you living on your purpose??? This is your mission.

To put it very simply, "Allow the God to give life to yourself first. And then you do unto others, as the God has been merciful enough to do unto you."

BEWARE OF THOSE WHO "CALL" THEMSELVES JEW, MUSLIM, AND CHRISTIAN, BUT "ARE NOT"

Now that our "Religious Confusion" is clearing out, and now that our "Spiritual Understanding" is re-surfacing, let us clearly comprehend one critical thing.

These religious titles of "Jew", "Muslim", and "Christian", are in fact just religious "titles" that are supposed *to describe the spiritual condition of a person's heart, mind, and therefore actions. Plain and simple. Simple and plain.* Please read that again.

Do not let these deceiving enemies further

deceive us from the common sense of understanding.

For example, the term "Jew" does not truly describe a separate race of people, as some caucasians would persuade us to believe. Listen. We all know that whitefolks is just plain whitefolks no matter what "religious title" they may try to use as a shield to hide the spiritual hypocrisy of their actions. Think about it analytically. The term "Muslim" does not truly describe a race of people either, as some caucasians would persuade us to believe too. All whitefolks is just whitefolks. Plain and simple. Simple and plain.

All these religions are arguing over different Gods, but they all agreeably share the same devil. They never argue over that.

These persons who have hypocritically labeled themselves "Jews", "Muslims", and "Christians" are the same caucasians that took part in The Slave Trade of Black Men, Black Women, and Black Children! The Same Ones!

Oh yes, you better make no mistake.

These are the same wicked "slave-traders", "slave-distributors", "slave-hunters", "slave-auctioneers", "slave-makers", and "slave-masters" that left hundreds of millions of us brutally murdered and extinct!!! And the ones of us who have survived physically, are suffering from such a state of mental-impairment inflicted upon us during this mental-rape, that we are considered to be mentally, morally, spiritually, and almost physically dead!!!

<u>These</u> <u>same</u> <u>so-called</u> "<u>religious</u>" <u>caucasians</u> <u>are</u> <u>the</u> <u>same persons</u> <u>who</u> <u>inflicted</u> <u>all</u> <u>of</u> <u>this</u> <u>evil</u> <u>upon</u> <u>us!</u> Yes they are! So, your intelligence should automatically tell you to beware of those caucasians who super-hypocritically <u>call</u> themselves "Jew", "Muslim", and "Christian". You better think about it.

They have not even attempted to "repent", "seek forgiveness", "sincerely apologize", "justly recompense", "humbly reconcile", let alone "seriously acknowledge" the tragedy that they have murderously inflicted onto a whole people.

This is because <u>obviously</u> and <u>historically</u> they have not been any angels of God (and are not angels today). Their history does not depict them to be any reflections of righteousness. Their own history shows them to have acted as aggressive enemies to fairness, justice, truth, equality, and righteousness. There is a consistent pattern of evil-spirited behavior here.

This people have historically acted in rebellion to God/Righteousness. Their thoughts and actions have reflected evil in the lowest form of mischief and the shedding of the blood of all peoples on every continent of this planet Earth. They maintain their world domination from the same wicked mind-state today. And their history is the consistent pattern of evidence that testifies to the spiritual dis-ease that is obviously infested within their hearts. As a man thinketh in his heart, so is he. As a man thinketh in his heart, so is he. As a man thinketh in his heart, so is he. So, who is he?

We must remember that Lucifer, Satan, Iblis, or the devil is not really some big ugly monster somewhere waiting to jump out and get us (because he already came and got us).

Lucifer is:

1.) just a scriptural picture of **a fallen angel** that is representative of "actual persons" in our present everyday lives...

2.) **"a person"** who has **fallen down** from a high state of righteousness, because of a spiritual sickness that has infected their heart...

3.) **"a person"** who **arrogantly refuses guidance** into a productive life of righteousness...

4.) **"a person"** who has knowingly made a **conscious decision to rebel** against righteousness or God....

5.) **a group of "people" who possess all of the characteristics above, but have unified and consolidated their wicked energy and efforts into one solid collective force in an attempt to** *oppressively dominate, and destructively manipulate the entire world's population for the purposes of their own selfish personal gain and personal pleasure, at the expense and demise of everyone else.*

You didn't hear that did you? Please read that over again, slowly. Study that. Study that, and then look around you. Study that, and then look at self.

Okay, but what is the point to all of this? Why is all of this being said? Listen closely beloved Blackman and Blackwoman.

If we do not want to be further "Religiously Confused" and "Religiously Divided", then we can not further take our religious instruction from those who are spiritually-ill.

Intelligence should naturally tell us not to take our instruction and guidance from those who do not have our best interest at heart.

They need instruction and guidance

themselves. The blind have been leading the blind, and now we have all fallen into the ditch of stupidity. We can't make the same mistake again.

Take your religious instruction or your spiritual guidance from an **"Original" Black Theological Perspective Only,** or else this religious confusion and division shall continue to exist and persist. Please understand this. Please receive this.

Listen very closely. History tells us that the recently-civilized caucasian man that has labeled himself as "Jew", "Muslim", and "Christian", has actually adopted these righteous titles which actually only describe the spiritual innate nature of The Righteous Black Original Man & Woman. These righteous titles have been adopted (or stolen) from me and you. You are That Original Jew or Hebrew. You are That Original Muslim. You are That Original Christian. Yes, it's true.

These righteous titles were stolen by persons

who only wish to convert themselves "in name" but not "in mind, spirit, heart, and action." Look at their history. Think about it brother and sister. Just think about it for your own self. Think about it for your own self.

_____

So now, after learning this truth, "**we**" have no choice but to increase our own intelligent mental perception through studious analysis.

We have no choice but to sincerely and critically analyze the mind, heart, and actions of our own selves and our own Black people, but especially of those caucasians who "call" themselves, "Muslim", "Jew", and "Christian".

And, this is only because they have historically proven to be enemies of righteousness. Their specific actions call for us to be specifically suspicious of specifically them.

You are not pre-judging them or being

"prejudice" by doing this. No. To "pre-judge" is to ignorantly judge a thing "before" you get an intelligent knowledge of the thing that you are judging. In this situation, that is not what you would be doing.

Although, what you would be doing is "re-judging" (or re-evaluating) caucasians, only "after" you have studied the historical pattern of actions they have made. You are judging "with" a knowledge of that thing, as opposed to judging "without" any knowledge of that thing. You are not "<u>prejudice</u>" (foolish). You are being "<u>re</u>-judice" (wise). Read that again too.

Yet, I don't want you to get crazy and think that caucasians are the only persons to beware of. Oh no, no, no. No, no, no, no. No. No, brother and sister. No.

You know that they have spread their rebellious pattern of thinking all around the world to all peoples at every seashore that they have ever set foot upon.

The whole human family has become an

entire house of rebellious evil, in an attempt to imitate and assimilate the western european value system and mind state. This is true. *{Yet when you really go deeper into the science of mind evolution, you will begin to understand that caucasian behavior has only been a sign, symbol, trial, lesson, or opponent that reflects and stimulates the (previously un-seen) weaker side of our own selves that we have to conquer, control, and master in order to evolve into the Higher States of Mind (Heavens), to bring some peace and order to our lives. But, we will deal with that issue later, as our understanding develops.}*

The root point to this conversation is to beware of "__all__" of those who shroud their wicked hearts in Righteous Garments whether they are black or white.

The only reason that caucasians are being singled out, is so that we may "study" their rebellious nature and character. Once you fully study or familiarize yourself with that behavior, you will be able to recognize those same mischievous characteristics coming from any person of any race, creed, color, or sex. It is really just the same little minded person masked in different exterior disguises. So, be aware of their presence and deal with them accordingly.

But most of all...most of all, we must be on guard against that same spiritual illness and those same evil characteristics within Self, Self, Self, and Self! That is the real challenge. The real challenge is to deal firmly with the hypocrisy of Self!

But, don't worry your mind too much though, because a truly good heart will always eventually (or event by event) guide us aright. A "truly" good heart will guide us aright. Always.

All things will work for the good of those who seek the good in all things.

And a good heart can perceive other good

hearts. The focus is not just for us to merely pay our attention to those who are impure in heart, or for us to become obsessed, paranoid, and threatened by their presence. No.

We only need to recognize them so that, if they will not change the condition of their hearts, we can get them out of the way of who and what we are really looking for. And we are really looking for our family "The Righteous".

Our focus is to re-unite the family that has been scattered and lost from one another (the lost sheep).

The true focus is to seek out these ones that are pure in heart, that we may commune (or reciprocally communicate) with them...and let their heart be in us...and our heart be in them. They will be in us, and we will be in them. Then we and our people will be One...again.

That is the focus. That is the "true" focus.

TRUE
SPIRITUAL
LOVE

TRANSCENDS ALL
RELIGIOUS DIVISION

Listen. The truth of this matter must be told. We must take a good look at self. Do you have the courage to take a long honest look at self through objective eyes? Do you have the courage to face the real questions? Let us see.

Now, think about this. In what ways are we creating and inflicting this same "Religious Confusion and Division" upon our own selves?

In what way is our own ignorance, envy, vanity, spiteful pride, or devilishment, contributing to the destruction of our own people?

Look, the truth is that, in all of our so-called "religious-convictions", and our so-called "spiritual-enlightenment", and our so-called "cultural-consciousness", we are still a Black community that is divided into little small minded cliques, factions, clubs, and schizims! AND ALL OF THIS IS VANITY! ALL IS VANITY!

We, so-called "enlightened ones" are supposed to be the ones of our community with some type of direction in life, but we are the ones in need of some direction and in need of some enlightenment! It is no wonder that the masses of our people are in the terrible condition that they are in, considering the childish silliness that goes on amongst the so-called enlightened community. Look at us.

The "religious-community" is walking

around reciting holy scriptures, but not living them. The "culturally-conscious-community" is walking around memorizing dates in Black History, but not making any Black History. It is all vanity.

And what is so tragically sad, is that all of this goes on while the masses of our people fall deeper into the pit of Hell to die.

But who is at fault for all of this division and "clique-mentality"? We have already talked about the hidden hand of the enemy, but what about our own Black hands? Yes, what about our own Black hands? Well? How much of this division in our community are we directly responsible for, our own selves? Let us have the courage to sincerely deal with these questions.

See, **in order for the enemy to manipulate us, the enemy must first find something within us to manipulate us with.** And we make it so easy for our enemy to array us into little oppositional cliques, because of our own deep self-hatred, plus the hatred of one another. Follow this now.

Listen, **an outsider could not walk up into your house and easily manipulate you into opposition against your own blood brother, unless somewhere deep down in your heart, there were already some feelings of opposition toward your brother in the first place.**

That's right. Do you understand? Read that again! Read it slowly.

If you have some hidden feelings of "jealousy", "envy", "mis-trust", or "hate" towards your brother, an outside force could easily use the illness of your own heart to tear apart the family unity in your own house.

You talk all of this religious talk, but there ain't no **love** in your heart! You talk all of this Black pride talk, but you don't **love** your people. Stop lying...no you don't! You don't even **love** yourself. Let's just tell the truth here.

This is why the enemy can so easily manipulate the Black community into opposition against itself. We are already sick with jealousy, envy, mis-trust, and hatred of self and one another. We have no true **love** for each other.

So, even with all of our "religious convictions" and even with all of our "revolutionary philosophies"...if we have not **loved**, we have done nothing. Nothing at all. Nothing.

But, **love** is not the true root of "your" striving. And "you" know who I'm talking to. I'm talking to "you". **Love** is not the true motivation of your heart, now is it?

Because, you and I know that a **True Love** for self and our people does not produce a "clique-mentality"! A **True Love** for self and our people does not allow an enemy to pit us against one another! A **True Love** for self and our people does not allow us to be divided over petty little surface labels and titles! A **True Love** for self and our people does not foster jealousy, envy, mis-trust, or hostility toward one another!

The truth is that, if we truly **loved** God and **loved** Righteousness, there would be no religious confusion nor division amongst us.

This is true because when "you" truly **love** Righteousness in "your" heart, "you" will **love** the doers of Righteousness; no matter what religious title they may proclaim, or even if they proclaim no religious title at all. Can you feel what is being said?

It is time that we just wake up from this childishness, and get to the real root of things. This is an emergency situation. Our people are being consumed by death as we speak, so now we need a basic root understanding. Let's look at it again.

When you truly **love** God you will **love** all those who **love** God and want to do The Righteous God's will. You won't care by what superficial "external" name they call God, as long as we are all striving to know God "internally" through the depths of an Understanding Wisdom. Think deeply about that.

See, a True Spiritual Love for God and The Righteous, is too big to be bound up within the lines of fractionalized division and a small-minded "clique-mentality". Real Love is too big for that.

Whenever you see persons who are "arguing" and "fighting" over "superficial religious lines of division", there is no true love there. There is no love for God, Self, nor Kind.

There is just a little small-minded heart full of ignorant hostility...looking for any vain reason to spew a bickering, hateful venom. No, there is no love there. But, where is the Love??? Where is that True Spiritual Boundless Love for God and Righteousness??? Well if we truly looked at the Spiritual Masters that we "claim" to already be looking at, we might find this Spiritual Love.

Imagine this for a second. Listen. A wise man once said that "...if Jesus, Muhammad, and Moses were all in this room together, they would embrace each other in brotherly love."

They would look into each other's eyes and begin to cry with eternal joy, recognizing the beautiful presence of The God illuminating from the pure heart of one another. They would look at each other and see self. They would see God reflecting through one another!

Jesus, Moses, and Muhammad, would emphatically Love one another in the spirit of true brotherhood! But the so-called followers of Jesus, Moses, and Muhammad, ignorantly hate one another in the spirit of evil and from the mind of ignorance!

This is precisely because they are not the "true" followers of either one of these representatives of God. They are only the fallen followers of their own vanity and they are the workers of their own inequity. Think about it.

Those who have understanding, and those who have love in their hearts, know that there is only one line of division. That line is drawn between the lovers of righteousness and the lovers of wickedness...the doers of good and the doers of evil. One to the left. One to the right. A perfect love. A perfect hate. Love one. Hate the other. Plain. Simple.

Blackpeople listen. Let us hear this goodly calling if we are truly of good. Let us consume this good news if we are truly seeking good.

Do away with this unjust hate for one another. Make love amongst yourselves and give birth to a Unity so strong that no enemy can destroy.

With a for-real love we shall have a <u>rock</u>-solid Unity. And on this Rock, we shall rebuild Our House...to stand firm throughout the infinite expanse of all time and all space. All that we have to do is say "Be", and it is. "Be", and it is.

SPIRITUAL
UNITY
FINAL WORD

Author's Note:

(Before we get started with this final word, let me ask those of you who have not read this entire book yet, to just go back to the beginning. Have a little patience.

Read the entirety of the writings. Don't be disrespectful. If you are truly seeking understanding, you will read each essay in the appropriate order. Yet, if you are foolish, you will just hastily disregard this note and continue to read this final word, assuming that you know something that you really don't. Only a fool will try to put on his shoes before his socks, so don't be backward.

Take your time, and read this one right. It is good that you are even interested enough to pick up this book, but wisdom don't come in no "microwave package". Okay? So, just go on back to the beginning and stop being so impatient. Go on. What you still reading for? Go on. I am not playing with you, go on. Go!)

"**Spiritual** Unity" is the opposite of "Religious Division". And "**Spiritual** Clarity" is the opposite of " Religious Confusion".

This is a new time, a new day, and a new age. You and I are now transcending "Religious Confusion" and "Religious Division", to attain "**Spiritual** Clarity" and "**Spiritual** Unity".

We will soon understand that "Religion" has simply served as an organized systematic structure of rituals centered around a particular philosophy or doctrine to assist us in keeping a righteous/spiritual frame of mind during this evil transitory world. Stop. Please read that over again.

We will soon understand that the "religious ritual" is just merely an "outer" sign or symbol of the "internal" heart and mind of a "spiritual" person who is in submission to righteousness. Stop. Please read that over again too.

We will begin to put less emphasis on the different outer religious rituals, and begin to put more emphasis on the internal righteous spirit of which the ritual is a sign of. We will transcend the many different "rituals" to the ONE "spiritual". The ONE "sphere - ritual".

This will be the final death of religious confusion. The wisdom of love will transcend it all.

I want us all to understand that this message of spiritual unity has been inspired by the circumstantial death, division, and destruction in our entire Black Nation Worldwide. Of course, we know that. But I also want to make it very clear that this message was given the life of expression, from the active ingredients within the teachings of Truth, given to us by The Honorable Elijah Muhammad through the words of our Brother Minister Louis Farrakhan. Please objectively understand this before unwisely condemning this.

I've watched this Blackman inspire, enlighten, motivate, and rally Blackpeople from all walks of life, at one time, in one place, with one spirit. It did not matter what little titles and labels we thought we had when we first walked into the auditorium, because by the time that we left, the word of truth had put us all on one accord. Our love for self and love for kind had out-grown all of our different little egotistical labels. That is Unity. That is Unity in action. That is an example of Love based on a common-unity. A community. A brotherhood. A sisterhood. Let no enemy tear us apart.

It does not matter so much about these different religious rituals and religious titles. The seasons are changing. Don't concern yourself so much with that anymore. A COMMON LOVE FOR TRUTH, WISDOM, and RIGHTEOUSNESS will transcend all of that today. The message of truth belongs to us "**all**" equally. So receive it, and allow it to multiply, deeply within yourself.

Out of the ashes of "Religious Confusion" and "Religious Division", shall arise the united beauty of "**Spiritual** Clarity" and "**Spiritual** Unity". This beautiful metamorphosis is occurring within you and I right now. So, let us grow it, feed it, nurture it, and mature it. And after we have re-developed into our own spiritual maturity, let us serve the world with the light/life that we have re-dis-covered. "Religious Confusion" is at death. "**Spiritual Unity**" is at hand.

I hope that you have enjoyed the reading. "Thank You" for your open heart, and for your open mind. Also, "Thank You" for your time. Continue to seek knowledge of your self.

Peace And Blessings
Be With Us All.

OTHER
RELEVANT READINGS

1. **STOLEN LEGACY**
   GEORGE G.M. JAMES

2. **AFRICAN ORGIN OF BIOLOGICAL PSYCHIATRY**
   DR. RICHARD KING

3. **OUR SAVIOUR HAS ARRIVED**
   HON. ELIJAH MUHAMMAD

4. **AFRICAN HERITAGE STUDY BIBLE**
   JAMES C. WINSTON PUBLISHING CO.

5. **HOLY QURAN**
   A. YUSEF ALI TRANSLATION

6. **MESSAGE TO THE BLACKMAN**
   HON. ELIJAH MUHAMMAD

7. **GOD, THE BLACKMAN AND TRUTH**
   (RAHBEE) BEN AMMI

8. **THE I CHING**
   WILHELM/BAYNES TRANSLATION

9. **SELECTIONS FROM THE HUSIA**
   MAULANA KARENGA TRANSLATION

10. **TAPPING THE POWER WITHIN**
    IYANLA VAN ZANT

11. **THE DESTRUCTION OF BLACK CIVILIZATION**
    CHANCELLOR WILLIAMS III

12. **THE ICEMAN INHERITANCE**
    MICHAEL BRADLEY

13. **SLAVERY: THE AFRICAN AMERICAN PSYCHIC TRAUMA**
    SULTAN ABDUL LATIF & NAIMAH LATIF

14. **METU NETER I & II**
    RA UN NEFER AMEN

15. **LIGHT FROM ANCIENT AFRICA**
    DR. NAIM AKBAR

Other Books By Author
Currently in Print

---

1. **"From Niggas to Gods Pt. 1"**

   Akil (250 pgs. Nia Comm./Press $12.95)

2. 12-Lessons To Restore The Image,
   The Character, & The Responsibility of:
   "The Goddess Blackwoman"

   Akil (170 pgs. Nia Comm./Press $12.95)

3. **"From Niggas to Gods Vol. II"**
   Escaping Niggativity & Becoming God

   Akil (301 pgs. Nia Comm./Press $14.95)